CW00486003

The Effective Team's

Knowledge Management

Workbook

By Elisabeth Goodman

RiverRhee Publishing

Published in the United Kingdom by RiverRhee Publishing, a trading name of RiverRhee Consulting Ltd, 49 Meldreth Road, Shepreth, Nr Royston, Herts SG8 6PS.

A CIP record of this book is available from the British Library.

First printed in November 2016.

ISBN 978-0-9926323-8-0

Printed in Great Britain by Cambridge Printers Limited

Contents

Acknowledgements

My journey into knowledge management began in the 1990s, when I was working at SmithKline Beecham and Tony Murabito joined us as the Head of the Information Management department. He was passionate about this relatively new discipline then, as he still is today. He gave me the opportunity, along with various colleagues including Dan Law, to co-ordinate a strategy for our department and for the R&D organisation as a whole. In 2001, I took what we had learned and applied it to a cross-R&D business change programme on knowledge management in the newly formed GlaxoSmithKline.

Working in that team with Helen Chapman and Jacqui Alexander (née Glossop) put me in touch with how they had been applying knowledge management in Glaxo Wellcome. I also had a unique opportunity to participate in a US study tour organised by Caroline Vance and Paul Ormerod at CEST (Centre for the exploitation of Science and Technology) that brought the different knowledge management practices to life.

More recently, I was programme events coordinator for NetIKX (Network for Information and Knowledge Exchange), which put me in touch with a wide community of knowledge practitioners, brought me up-to-date with the technology and tested the longevity of some of the core principles and approaches of knowledge management.

I also, thanks to Jackie Hunter, was able to test some of the ideas in the collaborative (or "Open Innovation") models in the Pharmaceutical Industry that we taught to senior R&D executives. Jackie also kindly wrote the foreword for my publication with John Riddell, "Knowledge Management in the Pharmaceutical Industry" with Gower. John's expertise in Communities of Practice first led me to get in touch with him at GSK, and he became my first Associate with RiverRhee. We were also able to involve a number of knowledge management practitioners as interviewees for our book, including Tony Murabito, and also Sandra Ward whom I have known since my earliest years in Information Management.

Knowledge management continues to be a cornerstone of my work with managers and teams in Library and Information Management and in the Life Sciences. It finds its way into most of my RiverRhee Consulting workshops, courses and one-to-one coaching sessions, even though I don't necessarily mention it by name.

This is the fourth of my workbooks for effective teams. My thanks go to Nathaniel Spain again for conceiving and creating the book cover illustration, and for his skillful rendering of the various other drawings that appear in this book as well as in my courses and blogs. Isabelle Spain has again helped me to create some compelling chapter headings. Jonathan Spain continues to be my greatest fan and enthusiastic co-author for the RiverRhee Publishing brand. Thank you.

Preface

We are all knowledge workers: we rely on our knowledge and expertise, and on what we can learn from others and their work to make decisions and to innovate. Why would the ability to capture, share, and explore what we have learnt not form the basis for generating new knowledge and so be integral to everything that we do?

Without it we risk repeating past mistakes, unnecessarily repeating work that has been done before, missing opportunities to leapfrog into new domains of knowledge.

Knowledge management is about deliberately putting in place principles, processes and tools that will enable us to make the most of the knowledge and expertise available to us. This knowledge is in our own and other people's heads. It is also documented in paper and electronic form. The challenge, for individuals, teams and for organisations, is to make this knowledge an integral part of how we work.

The ideal is to make it second nature to consider what we can learn from our own and others' experience before we begin a piece of work, at key points during this work, and when we have completed it.

A large part of knowledge management is simply about providing relatively simple frameworks to enable fruitful conversations to take place. For instance, an "After Action Review" happens at the end of any significant event: a milestone on a project, or a meeting. Participants are encouraged to reflect on what their goals were for the event, what actually happened, and what they can learn from that for future events or to share with others. It can be a simple and, at the same time, a very powerful conversation.

Like a lot of my approaches with teams, knowledge management encourages people to take some time to think about <u>how</u> they are working, in the interest of making their work more productive and enjoyable.

I will be describing the knowledge management frameworks and approaches in this book.

The use of technology to support knowledge management is potentially more complex. As technology is perpetually changing and others are far more expert in it than I am, I will not be attempting to document all that is available and how to use it. Instead I will be focusing on principles and practices that can be applied across different technology platforms.

The approach and format for this workbook is much like that of my previous three. It can act as a refresher for people who have attended one of my workshops relating to knowledge management, or where I have referenced some of the approaches. It can be used as a stand-alone manual for individuals who wish to learn about the different ways that they could apply knowledge management in their work. It can also provide the basis for planning and facilitating workshops with others.

Please note that this book is an introduction to the discipline, and you might want to read around the subject, take some formal training, or use an experienced practitioner to support and mentor you on your further journey. Do get in touch if you would like me to help you with that.

Each chapter is designed to reflect my approach for running workshops in knowledge. The first chapter helps you to create a definition of and language for knowledge management that will work for you, your team or your organisation. The subsequent chapters are best followed sequentially as they will take you through a step-by-step approach for shaping and implementing your own knowledge management strategy.

There are practical scenarios to show how the various principles and methodologies can be applied in almost any area of work. Each chapter has an exercise for practising the principles and methodologies, either in teams or individually. If you are using this book in teams, do allow plenty of time for the exercises and for discussion and reflection.

The workbook also includes support materials in the form of full-page versions of templates for use as a team and for your individual planning.

The material on each of the three scenarios is also consolidated at the end of the book.

Finally, there are references for further reading for those who would like to find out more about the subject.

Introduction to the Practical Scenarios

I will be using the following practical scenarios throughout the book to show how the various principles and methodologies can be applied. They are variations on the three that have I used in my previous books. They are partly based on real situations that I have encountered, but also adapted to better illustrate the points that I am making.

Scenario 1 – Running a centralised (shared) business service

A central library is responsible for core processes such as purchase of print and electronic resources, subscriptions and loans. It supports and is linked to a network of local libraries that interface with local business (or functional) groups. There are opportunities to share knowledge between the local and central libraries that will help the central library to run more effectively.

Scenario 2 – Enhancing the effectiveness of scientific projects

A Life Science team is responsible for carrying out internal research projects, and study-related projects for external clients. Applying knowledge management practices to the way it carries out its projects will enable it to enhance its performance.

Scenario 3 - Refocusing the approach of an SME (Small or Medium Enterprise)

This organisation has significant opportunities to grow through the exploitation of internal and external knowledge and expertise. It has a number of different options for how to do this.

Chapter 1. Choosing your Language

"Knowledge sharing is power"

Background and principles

What is knowledge management?

There is nothing new about sharing what we know. We do this every time we have almost any kind of conversation, or when we write an article or a report. We are passing on something that we have experienced or learnt, interpretations and conclusions we have drawn, decisions we have made.

And yet, in the 1990s, the discipline of 'knowledge management' emerged. Practitioners and advocates believed that we needed a more structured approach to ensure that all the knowledge generated within organisations was being used as fully as possible. They wanted to safeguard against it being buried in archives or technological systems, or lost to the organisation when key people left. There was a concern that people might want to hoard rather than share what they knew in the belief that "knowledge is power". And there was a worry that we would miss opportunities to use all the existing knowledge within an organisation as the rich basis for generating new ideas, and new knowledge.

Knowledge management was a multi-disciplinary approach that addressed all of these targets. Sometimes it sat within the Human Resources department of organisations, sometimes in Information Technology, sometimes in Library and Information services, sometimes in strategic departments. (More background on the origins of knowledge management can be found in the Further Reading reference at the end of this book.)

Nowadays opinion is divided as to whether knowledge management was just a fad, has become integrated into how people work, or still requires dedicated roles to make it happen. Many organisations do have roles and departments with formal knowledge management remits.

My own belief is that knowledge management should be an integral part of how we work and that we have to take active steps to initiate and sustain associated good practices. Sometimes specific roles or departments will be needed to make this happen, but ultimately it should be woven into the fabric of an organisation.

These are the definitions that my company, RiverRhee Consulting, uses in its work:

"Knowledge Management is a business philosophy. It is a set of principles, processes, organisational structures, and technology applications that help people share and leverage their knowledge to meet their business objectives." (after Gurteen).

By improving the way that you access, manage and use your internal information and knowledge your business can become a true 'learning organisation' and build on successes and new insights, rather than repeat mistakes and rely on out-dated knowledge.

We believe that a knowledge management strategy will only be successful if its objectives directly support those of the organisation, or are addressing issues that inhibit the organisation's growth and success.

Knowledge management terminology, principles, tools and approaches

Every organisation has its own common language for knowledge management. You will need to decide how you want to define it and if and how you will integrate it into the work of your team. As you read this and subsequent chapters, think about what vocabulary or language you would like to use to talk about knowledge management in your organisation.

Have an initial reflection or team discussion about the language you would like to use.   Figure 1.1 shows some of the knowledge management terminology in the form of a jigsaw. There is a blank version of the jigsaw at the end of this workbook that you could photocopy and use to build up your own language for knowledge management.

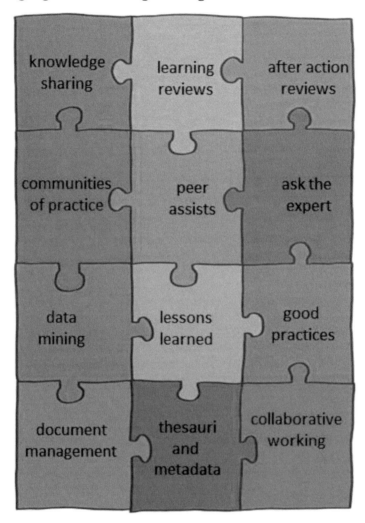

Figure 1.1 Example of an internal vocabulary for knowledge management

The mind set and principles for knowledge management

Knowledge management relies on a mindset that "knowledge sharing is power", that we should seek out what others know, and make what we know accessible to others.

Knowledge management can operate at multiple levels within an organisation. It can support strategic objectives, collaborations with external partners, projects, on-going processes, customer interactions, and the work of a team. I will explore this multiplicity in more detail in the next chapter when we will look at the different strategies that the three scenarios, and your own team might want to support.

There are three principles underpinning much of knowledge management. The first is that there is a knowledge cycle. The second principle is that of 'learning before, during and after'. The third is that knowledge can be shared in people to people interactions, as well as through people to 'content' interactions. (The content is represented in and subsequently retrieved from paper or electronic form.)

One way to represent the management of knowledge is in terms of the different phases of its existence, as shown in Figure 1.2

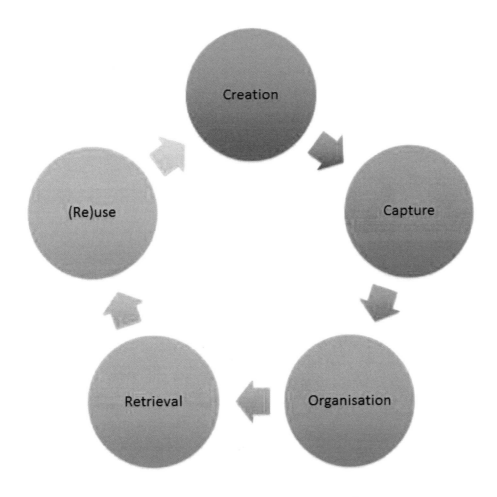

Figure 1.2 The Knowledge Cycle

New knowledge is created through research, experience, reflection, application and learning. This knowledge may come from one or more people working together. In order to be able to share knowledge, it must then be captured or recorded in some form – usually on paper or in electronic systems. Whatever medium the knowledge is captured in, it will require some kind of organisation so that it can be easily found again. Retrieval is the mechanism used to find that information. The cycle is completed when people are able to use, or re-use the information and apply it to improve their work, make decisions and generate new knowledge.

(You can read more about the distinction between data, information and knowledge; and also about the difference between 'tacit' and 'explicit' knowledge in the Gower publication, or other references cited at the end of this book.)

The next two principles expand on how to carry out each of the phases in the knowledge cycle.

Learning before, during and after
Many of the approaches used for capturing and sharing learning were well documented by Collison and Parcell in 2004, and are summarised in Figure 1.2.

You will have an opportunity to explore some of these approaches in more depth in Chapter 3 and beyond, but for now here is a reference to each.

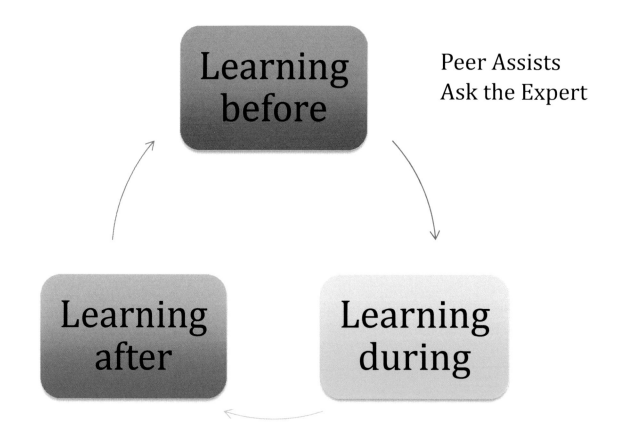

Peer Assists
Ask the Expert

Learning Reviews
(Lessons Learned)
Communities of Practice

After Action Review
(AARs)

Figure 1.3 Learning before, during and after

People to people vs. people to content interactions

Knowledge management approaches can be categorised into people to people vs. people to content interactions. People to people interactions rely on effective conversations (Figure 1.4): good listening and observation skills, open questions (using "why, what, who, when, where, how"), thoughtful answers and generous suggestions!

Figure 1.4 The art of conversation for sharing knowledge

Storytelling has also emerged as a popular modern-day technique for sharing knowledge. It is of course a very ancient technique that probably also dates back to our origins as hunter-gatherers, when it might have been used to share important lessons for survival.

The use of storytelling in your organisation could be something that you might like to explore further. A very basic framework is as follows:

- Think about the lessons or key messages that you would like the listener to come away with. Then construct a story around them.
- You might want to feature some characters, introduce them in a peaceful prelude, have something disruptive happen, describe what action they took, and have a happy resolution!
- Put in some sensory descriptors – sounds, sights, feelings and emotions to enrich your story and make it more vivid and memorable.
- The story could be based on something that happened to you or people that you know.

People to content interactions rely on the skillful capture and organisation of knowledge (Figure 1.5). Recorded knowledge can take many forms, for example:

- Documented procedures, with annotations to highlight good practices: what to do, or not to do based on the author's experience
- Short film clips demonstrating how to do something with a voice-over from the author
- A list of hints and tips, or replies to frequently asked questions (FAQs)
- Reports

Effective capture consists of ensuring that nothing vital is left out from the author's perspective, and also thinking about who might want to find the information and how they might look for it.

Figure 1.5 People to content – a way of sharing knowledge

Those of you who have roles relating to 'document management', or who create content for the web or for internal databases will have come across metadata: the data that sits behind, describes or indexes any document, image, or film clip and facilitates its retrieval by others. Metadata typically include a title, a short descriptive text, and a set of keywords (or tags), as shown in the example in Figure 1.6.

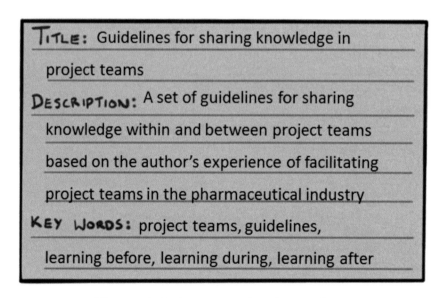

Figure 1.6 An example of metadata

Organisations sometimes develop thesauri: a list of standard key words to be used, so as to ensure consistency and guide people on the terms to use when looking for items.

Variations of these techniques are also used for organising data and information from scientific or technical fields of work in a way that facilitates 'data mining' or 'text mining'. This is the exploration and combination of data or textual information in often sophisticated ways that enables the generation of new knowledge. (There are some recent references at the end of the book citing examples of applications in Library and Information Management and in the Life Sciences.)

Closing thoughts

People to people interactions can also be described as a form of collaborative working: when two or more people work together to achieve a common goal.

This can be a short-term arrangement to achieve a specific task or a temporary one for a finite project within or across teams. It could also be a longer-term remit for an operational team.

Whatever the duration of a collaborative endeavour, it will be at its most effective when there is clarity about the goals, roles and responsibilities. It will also benefit from good working relationships, with active and open communication and well defined working (or good) practices.

Technology is often used to support collaborative working. Such technology can take the form of email, messaging systems, teleconferencing and video tools, intranets, document systems, databases and more.

Working practices for collaborative working might therefore include any of the following:

- Defining what technologies will be used for what purposes
- Agreeing on protocols for communicating when people are available for on-line conversations and when they need some privacy
- Editing and version control policies
- Central versus dispersed filing of electronic documents and associated ownership

What collaborative working practices do you have in place? How well are they working?

This chapter has introduced a lot of knowledge management principles and ideas. The next two chapters will explore the application of these principles and ideas to the three scenarios, and also help you to develop a knowledge strategy and tactics for your own organisation.

Chapter 2. Defining your Strategy

"Knowledge management should be an integral part of your goals and objectives"

Background and principles

Why practice knowledge management? What are the benefits?

People often ask how the benefit, or return on investment (ROI) of knowledge management can be measured or, even before that, how to get senior management to support it. My experience is that it only makes sense to practise knowledge management as an integral part of your individual, team or organisational goals. First clarify what those goals or objectives are, then explore if and how knowledge management can support them. Your return on investment is then measured in terms of the outcomes of those objectives.

Let's explore this in the context of the three scenarios:

Scenario 1 – Running a centralised (shared) business service

The central library is coordinating the purchase of print and electronic resources, subscriptions and loans on behalf of a network of local libraries. The local libraries are the interface with local business (or functional) groups.

There are a few ways in which the central and local libraries could pool their knowledge. For instance library staff in the local libraries will have a detailed knowledge of different customer groups and their requirements. Those in the central library will have a specialised knowledge of the processes involved in managing the central resources.

It is likely that all concerned will have strategic goals and objectives relating to the reduction of costs, and the increase of customer satisfaction.

The central library could benefit from the specialised knowledge of members of the local library. One individual might be the key contact, for example, for customers in a field of scientific research or a discipline such as Human Resources.

Scenario 2 – Enhancing the effectiveness of scientific projects

The Life Science team carries out internal research projects, and study-related projects for external clients, which are prime opportunities for applying knowledge management.

The long-term strategic objectives that these approaches could be addressing are for example reducing overall costs associated with the projects, reducing cycle time, increasing internal and external customer satisfaction. Short-term benefits might include the avoidance or reduction of risks associated with the project, or the grasping of otherwise unknown or ill-defined opportunities.

Scenario 3 - Refocusing the approach of an SME (Small or Medium Enterprise)

This organisation has significant opportunities to grow through the exploitation of internal and external knowledge and expertise. It has a number of different options for how to do this.

Again, the goals should be expressed first in terms of written objectives such as increasing the SME's market share, customer base or revenue by x%; being recognized as a centre of excellence in its field of research through rankings, invitations to speak, publications, patents; and so on.

SMEs typically build their knowledge base by recruiting experts to join their Advisory Boards, their senior management and scientific teams. Their staff members attend and speak at conferences, and the SMEs invite external speakers to give seminars. They read and publish papers. And of course they grow their internal bank of records and databases.

Individual or team exercise 2.1 What strategic goals or objectives could you support through knowledge management?

The strategic or organisational goals in the three scenarios include: increasing customer satisfaction; reducing costs; increasing revenue, market share and credibility or competitive edge.

Other goals might include:

- Complying with legal, regulatory, and health and safety requirements
- Innovation and continuous improvement
- Improved decision making

Or, for a team within an organisation, they could be:

- Strategic positioning within the organisation
- Influence and credibility
- Ongoing development of the department and of staff members
- An expanded network of contacts within or outside the organisation

Step 1

What strategic organisational or team goals should you be supporting?

How would knowledge management help you to enhance, reinforce or otherwise support those goals?

Are there any issues that are holding your organisation back? How could knowledge management help you with those?

How will you monitor or measure the success of your knowledge management strategy?

Use a mind-map to help you talk or think this through. Figure 2.1 is an example of how you might do this, based on a combination of the above scenarios. I have also included mind-maps for each of the scenarios at the end of the book.

Don't try to include specific tools and approaches yet. Chapter 3 will explore which ones you could use to tactically deliver your knowledge management strategy.

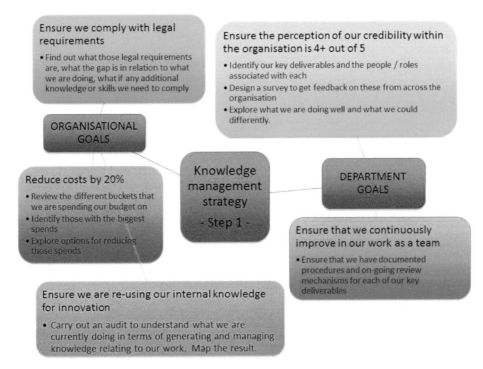

Figure 2.1 Sample mind-map for developing a knowledge management strategy

Closing thoughts

The mind-map that you have developed in exercise 2.1 is a starting point for reflection. Keep this to hand as you read through the next chapters of the workbook. It is likely that you will continue to revise the mind-map and your knowledge management strategy as you learn more about the options available to you.

Chapter 3. Selecting your Tactics

"Every strategy begins with tactics. Tactics work best on fertile ground."

Background and principles

You are now ready to consider what tactics will best support your strategy, and also best fit into your environment. For this, you will need some knowledge management approaches and tools. You will also need to consider where the opportunities exist to apply them.

What, if any, good practices for sharing knowledge and collaboration are already in place that you can build upon?

How could you best address any gaps?

What less helpful practices should be discontinued?

This chapter is about planning the tactics that will enable you to deliver your strategic goals and so enable the individuals and teams within your organisation to excel at what they do.

Chapter 4 will give you some ideas for practising the tools so that you can become more familiar with them before introducing them more widely.

Chapter 5 will help you to plan in more detail how to build and maintain engagement with your knowledge management strategy.

First, let me take you through a definition of each of the approaches and tools that you might use.

Detailed description of knowledge management "people to people" tools

Peer Assists

Teams can benefit enormously from taking some time to reflect about what they and others already know before starting on a new project or piece of work. 'Peer Assists' is a simple approach for doing just that.

As illustrated in Figure 3.1, Peer Assists consist of inviting people with relevant experience to a conversation about the new piece of work.

The host team considers what questions they might like to ask, and the invited team reflects on these before coming back with some answers and suggestions.

Peer Assists are a great way for the host team to get quickly up to speed on the challenges and opportunities to take into account in their new piece of work.

Figure 3.1 Host and invited teams in a 'Peer Assists' conversation

Ask the Expert

There will be individuals within and outside of your team who have a particular area of expertise that you would like to tap into. However they may have a limited amount of time to prepare a detailed presentation that is guaranteed to address all the questions you might possibly have.

'Ask the Expert' (Figure 3.2) provides an informal structure that minimizes the demands on the expert's time whilst ensuring that your team gets all or most of the answers that it needs.

As in 'Peer Assists', the team considers all the questions it might want to ask and invites the expert in. Each team member asks their question in turn, coming up with new questions as the conversation progresses, until they either run out of questions, or run out of time. If the expert does not know the answer, or does not wish to give it, they are free to say so.

It is amazing how much knowledge can be shared in this way, in a relatively short period of time. It is generally a very rewarding experience for the expert too.

Figure 3.2 An 'Ask the Expert' knowledge exchange

After Action Reviews

After Action Reviews are carried out immediately after any significant activity or event. They were adapted from US army practice and are typically used now at major milestones in a project, or at the end of a meeting.

After Action Reviews are an opportunity to reflect on what happened compared to the original goals, what can be learned from that, and what can be shared with others. They are designed to be quick and relatively informal. Above all, they should be treated as an open, "no blame" opportunity to learn and improve.

Typical questions are as follows:

- What were the original goals?
- What actually happened:
  - What went well?
  - What could have been improved and how?
- What have we learnt?
  - What actions will we take?
  - What can we share with others? With whom and how?

Learning Reviews and Lessons Learned

Learning Reviews are more in depth versions of After Action Review and are carried out at the end of a major piece of work. They usually benefit from some form of external facilitation as they take some time to set up, can involve quite detailed and sometimes sensitive conversations, and can require quite a lot of documentation and follow-up.

There is no single way of carrying out Learning Reviews, but approaches I have successfully used involve the following steps:

Step 1: An initial questionnaire or interview with all team members exploring questions that have been pre-agreed with the team leader. These might take the form of a team diagnostic as described in "The Effective Team's High Performance Workbook". Alternatively they might ask for reflections on the history of the work or project that was carried out in the style of what went well, what could have been done differently and how. A pictorial representation of the timeline of the work can often help to jog people's memory. The facilitator collates all the replies, anonymously if preferred, and reviews them with the team leader ahead of the next step.

Step 2: An interactive workshop with all team members is the opportunity to share all of the pre-workshop feedback. The discussion is carefully structured and the emphasis is on an open conversation, where all team members explore what they should ensure they repeat and what they could do differently in future work of this kind. They agree their next steps including sharing any knowledge with others.

Step 3: Lessons learned are a typical output from this exercise and there has been a lot of debate on how best to manage them. People often try to document them in databases, with a frequent consequence that these become a corporate 'black hole' never referred to again. I believe that the best policy is, as far as possible, to integrate lessons into documented procedures in the form of updates to processes, hints and tips, 'Frequently Asked Questions'

(FAQs) or good practices. 'Peer Assists' will also ensure that what has been learned is past on verbally from one team to the next.

Communities of Practice (CoPs)

CoPs are the final method in the 'Learning before, during and after' cycle. They are a way to connect people who work in related areas of knowledge and who are not otherwise connected within the organisational structure.

Their focus could be an area of technical or scientific expertise, an industry sector, a business or management skill, and so on.

CoPs typically have a charter, which includes any combination of the following:

- *A purpose or goal* – for instance to address a specific challenge or opportunity, or to provide on-going learning and development
- *An agreed format and frequency for their meetings* (face-to-face, virtual, monthly, quarterly etc.)
- *A typical agenda for their meetings*
- *Agreed methods* for preparing and documenting the inputs to and outputs from the meetings

CoPs ideally have the backing of a senior member of the organisation. They may continue on a long-term basis, or have a short lifetime, depending on their purpose.

Applying the knowledge management tactics

Let's explore the knowledge management approaches and tools that each scenario could use.

Scenario 1 – Running a centralised (shared) business service

The central library could use an Ask the Expert activity with individual members of the local library. Accessing their expertise about their customers' requirements would help with planning subscriptions for the next calendar year. This would also support discussions on how to best manage costs, and how to optimise customer satisfaction.

The central library could also conduct a Peer Assist with peer groups in external, non-competing, libraries. This would help them to explore alternative, cost-reduction approaches for managing subscriptions and loans.

Library staff in the different local libraries could set up a Community of Practice on the subject of how to best increase customer satisfaction.

The return on investment in these examples would be a comparison of the time spent in the knowledge sharing activities, compared to the reductions in costs, and to the increase in customer satisfaction.

Scenario 2 – Enhancing the effectiveness of scientific projects

The Life Science team could:

- *Conduct a Peer Assist* before starting on a new project to ensure that key learnings from other projects (what to do, or not to do, and how) are considered as part of the project plan and risk assessment.
- *Hold After Action Reviews* at pre-agreed project milestones (sometimes known as key decision points, or gateways) to ensure that any key learnings are being considered before moving onto the next phase.
- *Carry out Learning Reviews* at the end of projects to reflect on, address and share key learnings arising from these projects, and for future ones.

16

The Life Science team could consolidate its learnings in the form of documented or updated procedures. These could include lessons learnt, hints and tips or even video clips.

They could carefully apply metadata to electronic records to facilitate their retrieval.

They could also use data mining on existing records to discover new insights.

Teams working in geographically dispersed locations, or even within the same location would benefit from agreed collaborative working practices for managing their electronic information and their discussions.

Scenario 3 - Refocusing the approach of an SME (Small or Medium Enterprise)

Knowledge Management techniques that the SME could consider to make better use of its internal and external expertise include:

- *Structured Ask the Expert and Peer Assist* style conversations
- *Thoughtful use of metadata* in documenting their records
- *Data and text mining* on the records of their work
- *Encouraging good collaborative working practices* within and across teams to optimise how they share their knowledge and information

Individual or team exercise 3.1 What approaches or tools could you use to support your knowledge management goals?

Step 1

Take your mind-map from exercise 2.1, and review it against the approaches and tools available to you.

Which knowledge management approaches and tools will help you to deliver what you would like to do most effectively?
You could document this in the form of another mind-map, as shown in Figure 3.3.

I have also developed versions of this mind-map for each of the three scenarios, and you can find these at the end of the book.

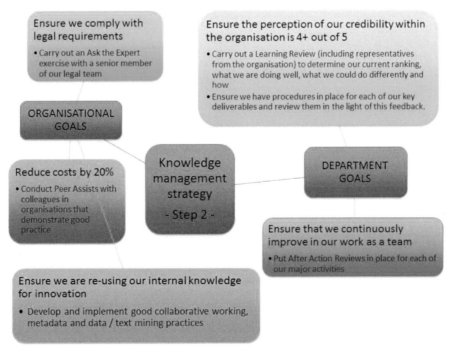

Figure 3.3 Sample mind-map for identifying approaches and tools

Having developed your second mind-map, on the approaches and tools that you might use to support your knowledge management strategy, it's time to start thinking about the practicalities of introducing these new ways of working in your team or your wider organisation:

- What, if any, good practices are already in place that you can build on?
- How could you best address any gaps?
- What less helpful practices should be discontinued?

Give these questions some initial thought and make a note of points that you would like to reflect upon further.

Closing thoughts

You now have a draft knowledge management strategy that is aligned with your organisational and/or department goals. There are some approaches and tools that you might use. You may have a mind-map or two to describe these.

You are also starting to develop the language that you would like to use around your knowledge management strategy – don't forget to update your jigsaw of terminology.

In the closing notes for Chapter 1, I referred to the various technologies available to support knowledge working and collaboration. Are there ways in which you could use the technology available to you in your organisation to support your goals?

Could you use the IT more effectively for collaborative working within your team, or with other teams? If so, are there working practices that you would like to define or improve in terms of how you manage online conversations, or offline discussions? What about how you file and manage different versions of documents and other media?

Would you like to use the IT for building stronger interactions with your customer groups? What kind of interactions would you like to support? How could you do so most effectively?

Could the IT be used in other ways than those you have thought of so far, for example to support management and retrieval through data mining or text mining?

It may take some effort and time to get the necessary buy-in from your IT department for the changes that you would like to make. Are there ways in which your objectives for knowledge management could be aligned with the IT department's strategies and priorities so that you could collaborate in delivering these?

Chapter 5 will help you with how to influence your colleagues in your own department, in IT, and in other parts of the organisation to get engagement for your plans.

But first, Chapter 4 will give you an opportunity to practise some of the knowledge management approaches and tools.

Chapter 4. Practising and Refining

> "It's easier to introduce people to new ways of working if
> you have experienced them yourself first."

Background and principles

It is always useful to have an opportunity to practise new ways of working, so that you know the 'ins and outs' of them before exposing others to them.

You can practise how to capture and share knowledge between people before starting new initiatives (learning before), at key milestones (learning during), and at the end of large pieces of work (learning after) in as little as 15-20 minutes.

It is similarly possible to get an idea of how to 'codify' or record areas of knowledge in a relatively short exercise.

These kinds of exercises will give you an idea of how the new ways of working could be applied in your organisation, and what guidance you would like to provide.

Practising knowledge management approaches and tools

Most of the following exercises are best done within teams, or groups of people, although the journalist's notebook, and practising metadata could be done individually or in pairs. Allow 15-20 minutes for each exercise, or longer if you wish.

Team exercise 4.1 Hobbies or pastimes – Ask the Expert

Invite each person to briefly state a hobby or pastime that they enjoy, using a one sentence description at most.

Make a note of each hobby or pastime on a flip chart. Invite people to vote on the top third that they would like to hear more about (other than their own!). So, for example, if there are six items, give each person two votes. They can put their votes on the same or different items on the list.

Choose the one or two hobbies or pastimes with the most votes, checking with the person that they belong to that they are happy to talk about it.

Arrange chairs in a semi-circle facing 'the expert'.

Ask each person in the semi-circle to ask the expert a question in turn, thinking of a new question if theirs has been taken.

Give the expert permission to say 'I don't know', or 'I would rather not answer that question'.

Ask them to only answer the question itself and then wait for further questions to expand on the topic more fully.

Conduct a debriefing exercise at the end to ask the expert, and the rest of the group about their experience with the approach and if / how they might apply it in their work. You could use the questions for an After Action Review, as described in Chapter 3, to do this.

Team exercise 4.2 The pajama game

Invite people to consider the aspects of their work in which they have expertise, and those in which they have a challenge that they would like some help with.

Prepare some pieces of paper, or post-it notes, in the shape of pajama tops and bottoms, and a piece of string with something suitable to clip the pajamas to it.

Ask people to write their individual areas of expertise onto separate pajama tops, and their challenges onto pajama bottoms.

As far as possible, match areas of expertise in the tops to challenges in the bottoms and clip the matching sets on the line, as shown in Figure 4.1

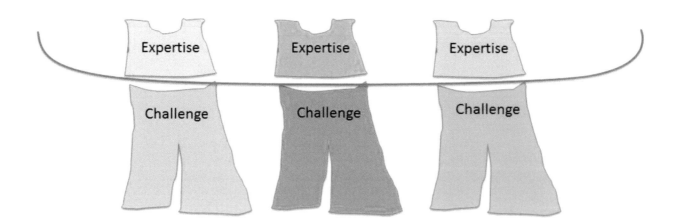

Figure 4.1 The pajama game

Decide as a group how you would like to explore the matching pajama sets. If several people have the same challenge, but only one person has the matching expertise, then this will lend itself to an Ask the Expert discussion, as described in Exercise 4.1.

As this is a work-related exercise, you might like to schedule some time on a separate occasion to discuss each topic more fully.

If two or more people have the same or a related area of expertise, and two or more have the same or a related challenge, then the discussion could take the form of a Peer Assist exercise.

Use the description of the Peer Assist in Chapter 3 to practise doing this in 15-20 minutes. Or, again, if you prefer, schedule some time on a separate occasion for a longer exercise.

On the other hand, you may find that you only need one-to-one discussions for the matching pajama sets in which case the journalist's notebook approach, described in Exercise 4.3, might be the most suitable.

Lastly, if there are several people with the same area of expertise, you might like to simulate a Community of Practice using the goldfish bowl in Exercise 4.4.

Whether you carry out an abbreviated or longer version of Ask the Expert, or Peer Assist, for this exercise, or any of the other approaches below, make sure that you allow some time for reflection on how things went, and how you would apply the approach more widely in your team or organisation. Again, you could use the After Action Review questions from Chapter 3 to structure this reflection.

Individual or team exercise 4.3 The journalist's notebook

The journalist's notebook (Figure 4.2) is something that you might already use to take notes about something you have learnt, or something that you would like to do.

Figure 4.2 The journalist's notebook

Think about how you could use your 'journalist's notebook' as a knowledge management tool. It could be in paper form, or in electronic form. It could be on your phone, a touchpad or your computer. You might use drawings or images, a mind-map, sound or video recordings.

There is some good software out there and apps especially for this kind of activity. Think about what works best for your style of learning.

What approach will you take to investigate an area of expertise: will you be interviewing someone and/or observing how the expert goes about what they do?

You might of course be speaking to or observing more than one person. You could make a note in advance of some starting questions that you would like to ask, or the aspects that you would like to observe. These are likely to evolve as you get into the interview or observation.

You could also define some colour coding or symbols to use so that key aspects that you want to remember will stand out.

There is a blank 'notebook' page at the back of this workbook that you could print copies of if you would like to play with that format.

The approach that you use for this kind of investigation, if you do it more than once, will probably evolve over time. Again, give yourself the opportunity to review how you get on, and how you can improve on your technique.

If you are the expert on something that you believe would be worth sharing and recording for wider use, why don't you find someone to interview and observe you? This person could be a new recruit in the organisation, or a member of your department or team that is interested in being cross-trained. Have them record what they learn from you, and then review their notes to add further detail as appropriate.

The goldfish bowl (Figure 4.3) is an enjoyable way to simulate and observe what might happen in a Community of Practice.

Figure 4.3 The goldfish bowl

To do this, first find a topic that several people would like to explore, and ask those with some expertise in the subject to gather in the centre of the room (the goldfish bowl). They can sit if they wish. Make sure that there are a few people left to stand or sit around the outside.

The topic could be, for instance, what project management methodology to adopt as standard practice within the organisation. The people gathered in the centre would then be those who have some expertise and/or experience in managing projects.

Ask the people in the centre to begin discussing the topic, whilst those on the outside take notes on the conversation. Once a few ideas have been discussed, and perhaps some decisions made, reverse the groups, so that the people who were on the outside of the goldfish bowl now come into the centre, and recap the main points they heard.

You can then, as a whole group, review how the conversations went, perhaps in the style of an After Action Review. Use this review to also reflect on how the experience could be extrapolated into a Community of Practice in the area of expertise involved, or indeed in any other areas of expertise within your organisation.

Note that you would not necessarily use the goldfish bowl approach in an eventual Community of Practice. Those who were in the centre of the goldfish bowl would usually be those forming the community.

The purpose of the outer circle was simply to assist in the observations and reflections of what happens when a group of 'experts' get together to explore a topic.

Team exercise 4.5 Learning Review

There is no quick and easy way to simulate a learning review, but you could experiment with one within your team as follows:

Step 1: choose a project or task that you carried out over a period of time, and create a visual representation of the timeline involved. An example of how you could represent this timeline is shown in Figure 4.4.

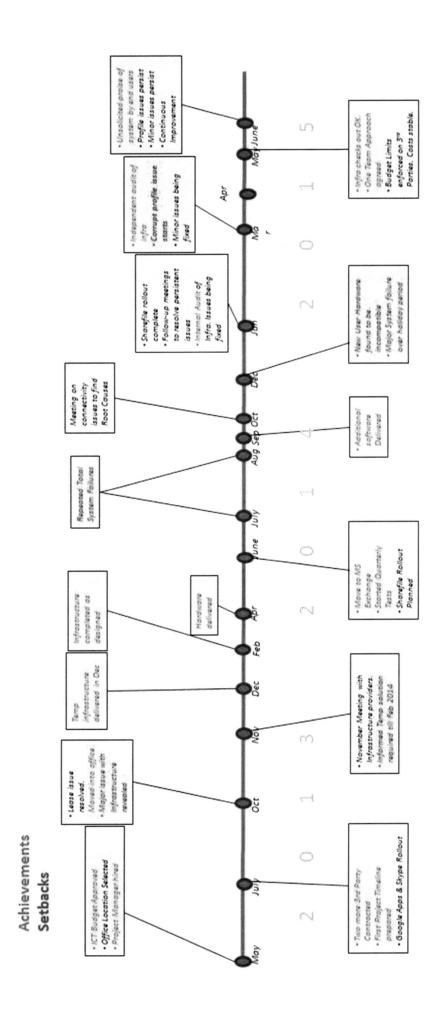

Figure 4.4 Example of a project timeline from a Learning Review with a London-based start-up company

23

Step 2: think about the types of questions that you would like to explore around what happened, and how you would like to ask them. Do you want to ask some simple questions about what worked well and what could have been done differently at each stage, or would you like to go into some more detailed investigation of how you worked as a team over time?

Do you want to give people the opportunity to answer the questions anonymously, verbally, in writing, before or during a face-to-face discussion?

Prepare to gather the responses appropriately.

Step 3: if you collected replies to the questions ahead of the face-to-face discussion, collate and summarise them in a form that will be easy for people to read and digest.

Step 4: agree the goals of the face-to-face discussion and how you will run it. Visuals, flip-charts and post-it notes are all useful props, as well as templates for recording outcomes and next steps.

It also helps to split into pairs or three's rather than to work as one large group.

Allow some time at the end to share and review outputs from discussions, agree on next steps, carry out an After Action Review, and reflect on how you can extrapolate this approach to the wider organisation.

Team exercise 4.6 Collaborative working

John Faulkes and Ralph White of PPMLD have a number of exercises that they use to simulate collaborative working. Here is one that I especially like and that you could try. They call it "Mountain Rescue" (see Figure 4.5).

Figure 4.5 "Mountain rescue" – an example of collaborative working

The brief for the facilitator:

1. Set up three to four tables, each one metre apart, in a large room. Each table represents a mountain peak. Each gap is a chasm between the peaks.
2. Place some small toy cars or lorries tied together with string at the furthermost table. This is the rescue convoy.

3. Put a group of small toy figures on the nearest table. The figures should be able to fit into the cars or lorries. They are the people to be rescued.
4. Have a plentiful supply of newspaper and tape, some scissors and a length of string. (You may deliberately see to it that there are not enough pairs of scissors etc. to go around.)
5. Split the group into teams - this works best with 12-25 people, with one team allocated to each gap between the tables.
6. Give each team a copy of their brief, and 25 minutes to complete their task. You may respond to questions that they ask. Observe how they behave and prepared to conduct a debriefing discussion at the end.

The brief for each team:

1. Your goal is to rescue the stranded people, using the rescue convoy and take them back to the vehicle starting point.
2. Each team must build a bridge across their designated gap, only using paper and tape.
3. Once all the bridges are built, one person will be pulling the vehicles from the starting point (using the length of string), and then back again to the starting point. No-one must fall off!

The debriefing discussion from the facilitator (do not share this with the team until after the exercise has been completed!):

1. What was the goal of the exercise?
2. What actually happened?
   a. What went well?
   b. What could you have done differently and how?
3. What have you learned?
   a. What action(s) will you take?
   b. What will you share with others?

Did the team:

A. Keep the goal in mind?
B. Work collaboratively rather than competitively – how did that manifest itself?
C. How did people communicate: did they listen to each other and consider all ideas? Did they share good practices between teams?
D. Did they consult with the sponsor / facilitator?
E. Did they agree any working practices for their teams?

Additional tips for the facilitator:

1. Do not allow the teams to put any extra supports under the bridges – there are very deep chasms beneath them
2. If they ask you questions such as whether they may work with the other teams – the answer is 'yes'
3. If one bridge fails, then the whole rescue operation fails!

Individual or team exercise 4.7 Practising metadata

Use the metadata templates at the end of the book to practise generating your own metadata for some types of knowledge that you would like to share in your organisation.

Put yourself in the mind of those who might want to find the information. Think about what your common keywords might be.

What have you learnt from this exercise?

How could you agree and manage a consistent use of metadata across the organisation?

Would creating a thesaurus help you?

Closing thoughts

I hope that you have enjoyed practising some of the tools in this chapter, and have been able to consider which ones might fit best into your team or organisation's working practices and how.

Hopefully you are now equipped with a set of hints and tips, or guidelines to support you and others in the use of the approaches and tools that you think will work best.

Take another look at your mind-maps for your knowledge management strategy and the approaches and tools that you will use. Review your jigsaw of terminology and any other notes you have made. Update these documents as appropriate.

You are now ready to move onto the next chapter, which is about building and maintaining engagement for your knowledge management strategy.

Chapter 5. Engaging your team

"Working practices only become such when they are <u>the</u> way of doing things."

Background and principles

The first and last steps for introducing any new way of working involve assessing how well people are likely to become engaged and how to build and sustain that engagement.

There are many ways to build engagement but it's a good idea to begin by assessing the current situation.   In this chapter I will take you through how to do this, and the things you can do to build and maintain engagement.

Evaluating the current situation

Think back to the knowledge cycle and the learning before, during and after models in Chapter 1. What are people's current attitudes towards these kinds of principles in your organisation and towards sharing knowledge in general?

What about their attitudes towards recording knowledge in a way that can be re-used, and towards accessing existing knowledge?

How receptive are they likely to be to some of the approaches and tools that you would like to introduce?

What if anything is already happening that is related to your knowledge management strategy that you could build upon?

What opportunities can you see that might help you to get started? What threats might get in your way?

A very simply way to evaluate the current situation is by means of a SWOT (Strengths, Weaknesses, Opportunities, Threats) analysis as shown in Figure 5.1

STRENGTHS

- Knowledge is a major input and output to our organisation's work
- There is already some form of knowledge sharing and collaboration going on
- Knowledge has a fundamental role in many of our processes e.g. Project Management, Collaboration / Alliance Management

WEAKNESSES

- Some people regard knowledge management as a bit of a fad
- There is scepticism about Return on Investment (ROI)
- It will take time and effort to make this happen

SWOT analysis for knowledge management in your organisation

THREATS

- Subject experts might be reluctant
- The organisation has some higher priorities
- It can be difficult to get / maintain senior management attention
- It could be perceived as too difficult / costly to do
- Previous related initiatives have 'failed'

OPPORTUNITIES

- It could facilitate other strategic goals
- The existing culture (of creativity, innovation, continuous improvement) could support it
- It will help us to better predict the likelihood of successes / failures in our work
- We have potential allies e.g. in HR, Communication, IT..

Figure 5.1 Example of a SWOT analysis for a knowledge management strategy

Individual or team exercise 5.1 – SWOT analysis

Carry out your own SWOT analysis on your knowledge management strategy, using the template at the back of the book.

If, as you do the analysis, you think that some people or departments might respond significantly differently, either make a note of these differences in the SWOT analysis, or complete separate analyses for the different people or departments.

Identifying ways to build and maintain engagement

I have written a separate book "The Effective Team's Change Management Workbook" on ways to lead change in an organisation. John Riddell and I also devoted a chapter on enabling change in our book "Knowledge Management in the Pharmaceutical Industry".

There are many other guides and methodologies for enabling change, and I am currently working with my committee members in the APM (Association for Project Management) Enabling Change SIG (Specific Interest Group) to produce an introductory guide to this whole area.

So my thoughts on the main ways to build and maintain change are constantly evolving. Readers would do well to form their own impression of what has worked best in their experience.

For now, here is my latest take on the subject:

1. *Clearly articulate your knowledge management strategy,* how it supports your organisation's or team's vision and the anticipated benefits. This is something that you have been working on since Chapter 2 in this book. You can also develop an 'elevator pitch' to help you succinctly describe your strategy in conversations with others. An elevator pitch is based on what you could say in a couple of minutes if you happen to find yourself in a lift (or elevator) with one of your stakeholders. I will walk you through how to develop your elevator pitch in the next chapter.

2. *Find opinion leaders and senior managers* who will speak for your knowledge management strategy, help you to resource it, and act as role models for it. If possible, get their backing to reward good knowledge working practices and to escalate non-compliance with agreed practices.

3. *Focus on the behaviours and attitudes that you would like to change*, and what will motivate people to adopt the new ways of knowledge working. Understand that different people (stakeholders) will respond differently and spend time with them to understand and plan your responses to those differences.

4. *Shape all the communication, training and support mechanisms* that you put into place around the behaviours, attitudes and motivators of your various stakeholders. Use any trusted project or change methodologies in your organisation to plan and deliver the communication, training and support. Pilot the new ways of working and publicise early success stories.

5. *Work as a team* to deliver your knowledge management strategy. Keep reviewing how you're going about it. Reflect on what's working and what you could do differently. Be role models for the knowledge management approaches and tools that you would like others to use.

6. *Monitor and share the benefits gained* (in the form of success stories and reports) and adjust your strategy accordingly.

Illustrations of engagement strategies from the scenarios

Here is how the engagement strategies for the three scenarios could be designed.

Scenario 1 – Running a centralised (shared) business service

I defined the potential knowledge management strategy for this scenario in Chapter 2. It focused on accessing the specialised knowledge of the staff in the central and local libraries, and learning from the expertise of similar organisations. This would help with the annual review of subscriptions and the streamlining of processes for subscriptions and loans in order to reduce costs and increase customer satisfaction.

Senior managers will be able to ensure that the strategy is reflected in departmental and individual objectives, and that people's performance is evaluated and rewarded accordingly.

Senior and middle managers will also ensure that knowledge-sharing activities are seen as a priority and that time is set aside to carry them out effectively.

Managers might even take part in or attend some of the activities and cite them as examples of good practice when talking to other members of the department or organisation.

The teams involved could document guidelines and then continuously review and improve on them after each round of knowledge sharing is completed so as to benefit from the lessons learned.

The knowledge strategy and how it is progressing could be a standing item on the teams' agendas, to provide updates on progress and the benefits gained.

Scenario 2 – Enhancing the effectiveness of scientific projects

The knowledge strategy for this scenario consisted of supporting the reduction of overall costs associated with the projects, reducing cycle time, and increasing internal and external customer satisfaction.

There were also short-term benefits to be gained such as avoiding or reducing risks associated with projects, and enabling the grasping of otherwise unknown or ill-defined opportunities.

The strategy included carrying out learning before, during and after interventions on new, existing and completed projects. It also included embedding the lessons learned in documented procedures, using metadata to index records, using data mining and developing collaborative working practices.

This is quite a broad range of activities to encourage and support, so the management team could support the strategy by recruiting or training a dedicated knowledge management resource. This resource could be a single person, or a small team depending on the pace and scale at which the organisation would like to progress.

The individual or small team could then work with representatives across the business to develop and then implement the new ways of working. This would be a good way to build success stories or case studies and perhaps to also cultivate opinion leaders to help spread the message across the organisation.

Understanding and adjusting the approach for implementation based on different stakeholders' attitudes and skills will be beneficial.

It will also be important to make the knowledge strategy part of everyone's objectives to ensure that there is a commitment across the board to adopt it.

If there is a small team or if a set of representatives is used to design and implement the knowledge strategy, then it will be important to spend time helping them achieve high performance.

Some form of team start–up event, with visible endorsement by senior management, will help with this. The start-up agenda could include time to:

- Articulate the vision and the anticipated benefits
- Develop the plan of approach
- Agree how the team will monitor and review its progress and generally manage its interactions and activities.

Scenario 3 - Refocusing the approach of an SME (Small or Medium Enterprise)

I suggested that this organisation could use a range of knowledge management techniques to make better use of its internal and external expertise.

As with Scenario 2, the complexity involved might benefit from the support of a dedicated individual or of a small team with representatives from the different parts of the organisation.

Support from the senior managers will be essential given the significant cultural change involved in transitioning from an academic to a more business like organisation. The managers will need to be seen to actively endorse and model the knowledge sharing and collaborative working approaches. They will be expected to act on any escalations of non-conformance, and to acknowledge and reward examples of good practice.

Other tactics include those described for Scenarios 1 and 2 such as:

- The use of explicit performance objectives
- Sharing success stories
- Cultivating opinion leaders
- Developing guidelines for training and support
- Embedding good practices within documented procedures and so on.

Individual or team exercise 5.2 – develop your own engagement strategy
Review your SWOT analysis from Exercise 5.1.

Which methods for building engagement could you use to build on the strengths, address the weaknesses, take advantage of the opportunities and mitigate the threats?

Develop your engagement strategy accordingly!

You might want to add this to your mind-maps from Chapters 2 and 3, or even develop a new one.

Check that your terminology is still as it should be, or revise it accordingly.

Closing thoughts

You should by now have a good idea of your knowledge management strategy and a plan for its implementation. You might even have begun putting it into place.

Remember that any activity involving how people work and interact with each other will be very dynamic and have variable rates of success.

Some of your plans may catch-on like wildfire and achieve a momentum of their own. Others might not work out quite as you had planned, and yet others might seem impossible to achieve.

Be philosophical and pragmatic.

Keep talking to your senior managers and to your other stakeholders.

Focus and build on what's working, and learn from what isn't. Keep things constantly under review, which brings us to Chapter 6.

Chapter 6. What Happens Next?

"The journey of knowledge sharing and personal enrichment is one that continues for life!"

Background and principles

You are now ready to review how you have shaped your knowledge management strategy.

You can:
1. Identify the departmental, site, global objectives where knowledge management can add benefit (look at your mind-maps, and jigsaws)
2. Explore the strengths, weaknesses, opportunities and threats of your current approach (look at your SWOT analyses and the engagement strategies)
3. Consider the knowledge sharing and collaboration approaches that would work best in your environment
4. Think about how you could influence people to take up the new ways of working

Remember: knowledge management is an enabler for business process improvement, for innovation and for decision-making. But it takes people to make it happen. Technology alone will not work!

Once you have reviewed your strategy you could articulate it in terms of an elevator pitch.

Individual or team exercise 6.1 – develop your elevator pitch

There is no single method for developing and articulating an elevator pitch, but here is one possible way to do so:

Step 1: consider all the possible answers to the following questions – write them on a flip chart:

a. Who are your target stakeholders?
b. What requirement(s) do they have to help them with their work?
c. What knowledge management intervention will help to address this?
d. What will be the resultant key benefit?

Step 2: work your statements into an elevator pitch sentence. This may take a few attempts and, if doing this in a group, someone might volunteer to draft some alternatives 'offline' and circulate them for review.

The elevator pitch will read something like this for each of the scenarios:

Scenario 1

"Our library staff in the central and local libraries would like to make better use of their expertise during the annual review of subscriptions and for how they go about subscriptions and loans generally. We will teach and facilitate some exercises that will help staff members to share their knowledge, and tap into that of external colleagues so that they can reduce costs and increase customer satisfaction."

Scenario 2

"Our scientists and senior managers would like to feel confident that they are making the best use of our internal knowledge when initiating and managing projects for external customers. We will coach and support project teams to use learning interventions at the start, during and at the end of all projects so that we can, as far as possible, reduce the cycle time and cost of our projects, and consistently ensure customer satisfaction."

Scenario 3

"We need to find ways to transition from being an academic to a more business like organisation. We will be introducing a range of knowledge sharing and collaborative approaches that will enable us to make better use of our internal and external expertise in order to facilitate and support that transition."

Now over to you!

Concluding thoughts

There's not a lot more to do now. If you have not yet thought about measuring and reporting on the benefits being gained from your knowledge management strategy, then think about this now.

As I said in Chapter 2, the chances are that the benefits from your strategy will be closely tied to the anticipated benefits from your organisation's overall strategic goals. So the benefits might be measurable in terms of cost reduction, time reduction, increase in quality or some variation of these.

How will you measure the benefits from your knowledge management strategy?

What indications if any are you already getting of the impact?

What if any adjustments will you need to make as a result?

The section on 'Control' in my publication "The Effective Team's Operational Excellence Workbook" (see reference below) has some helpful suggestions on different ways to measure impact.

A mind-set of knowledge sharing and on-going learning can be personally very rewarding. What would you like to do next?!

Here are the details of my other books for effective teams. The first three are published. The last one should be coming out in 2017.

"The Effective Team's Change Management Workbook" (2013) ISBN 978-0-9926323-5-9

This will help you to appreciate personal journeys, reactions and resistance to change and the processes to use when planning and implementing various types of change.

"The Effective Team's High Performance Workbook" (2014) ISBN 978-0-9926323-6-6

This will help you to explore the team development journey, tools for valuing the individual, defining the team's purpose and goals, self-evaluation of the team, and developing good working practices.

"The effective Team's Operational Excellence Workbook" (2015) ISBN 978-0-9926323-7-3

This will take you through a systematic approach for defining and improving how your team spends its time and resources, by ensuring that you are focusing on the right priorities to deliver value to your customers, and that your processes are simplified and streamlined.

Finally, "The Effective Team's Facilitation Workbook" will give you tools and techniques for stimulating your team's creativity in one-off exercises, half and one-day workshops, or when engaged in projects.

I would be very interested to hear of any feedback or questions that you may have on any aspect of enhancing team effectiveness.

Please get in touch at publishing@riverrhee.com

Full Page Versions of Materials for Use in Workshops

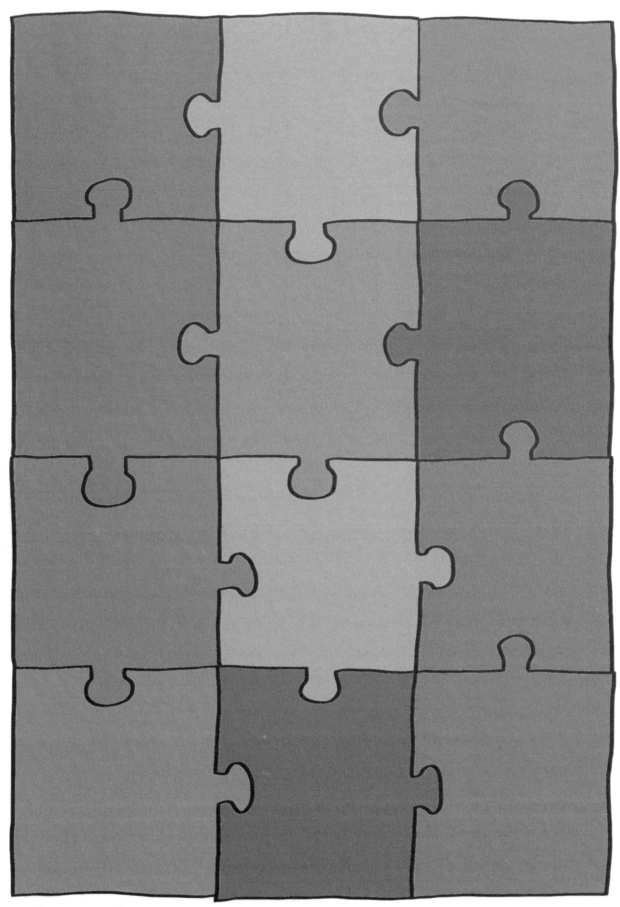

Jigsaw template for creating your own knowledge management terminology

Taken from Chapter 1 Choosing your Language – in "The Effective Team's Knowledge Management Workbook", RiverRhee Publishing, 2016

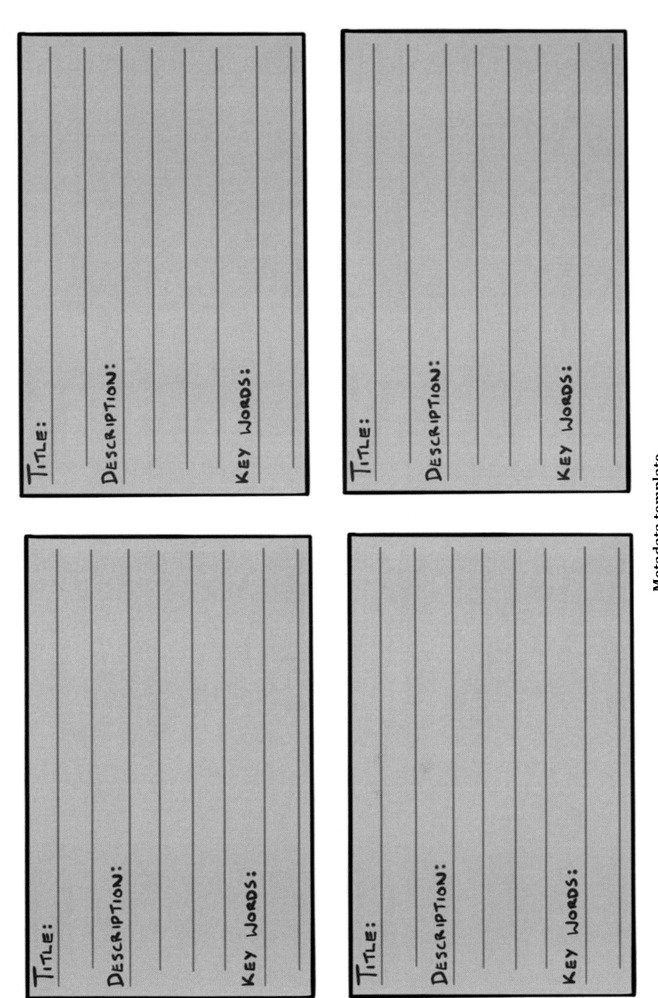

Metadata template

Taken from Chapter 1 Choosing your Language – in "The Effective Team's Knowledge Management Workbook", RiverRhee Publishing, 2016

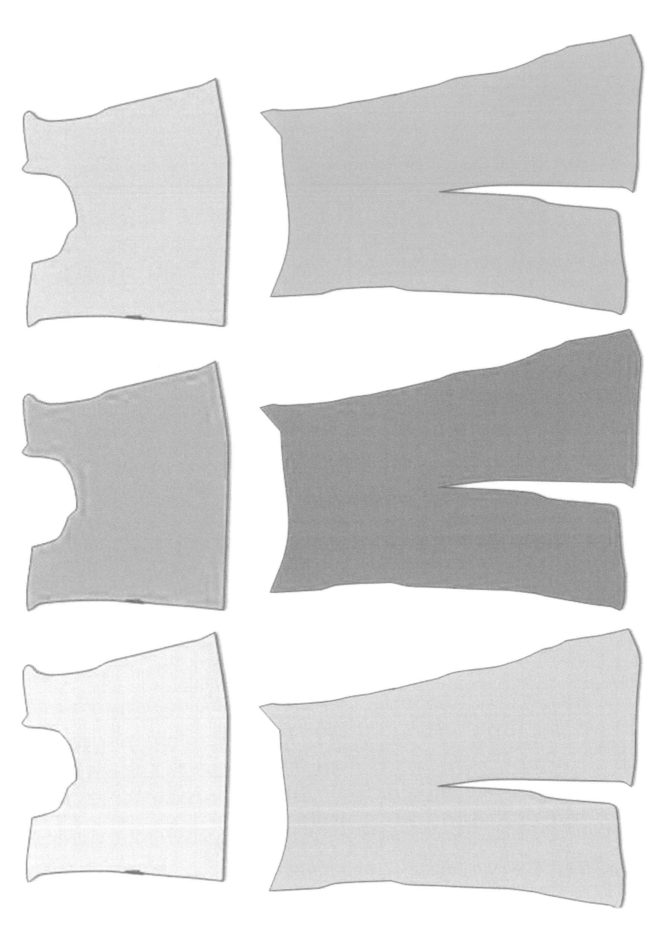

Pajama tops and bottoms for the knowledge marketplace exercise

Taken from Chapter 4 Practicing and Defining ... "The Effective Teacher ...

Journalist's notepad for noting Q&A for knowledge sharing conversations

Referenced in Chapter 4 Practising and Refining – in "The Effective Team's Knowledge Management Workbook", RiverRhee Publishing, 2016

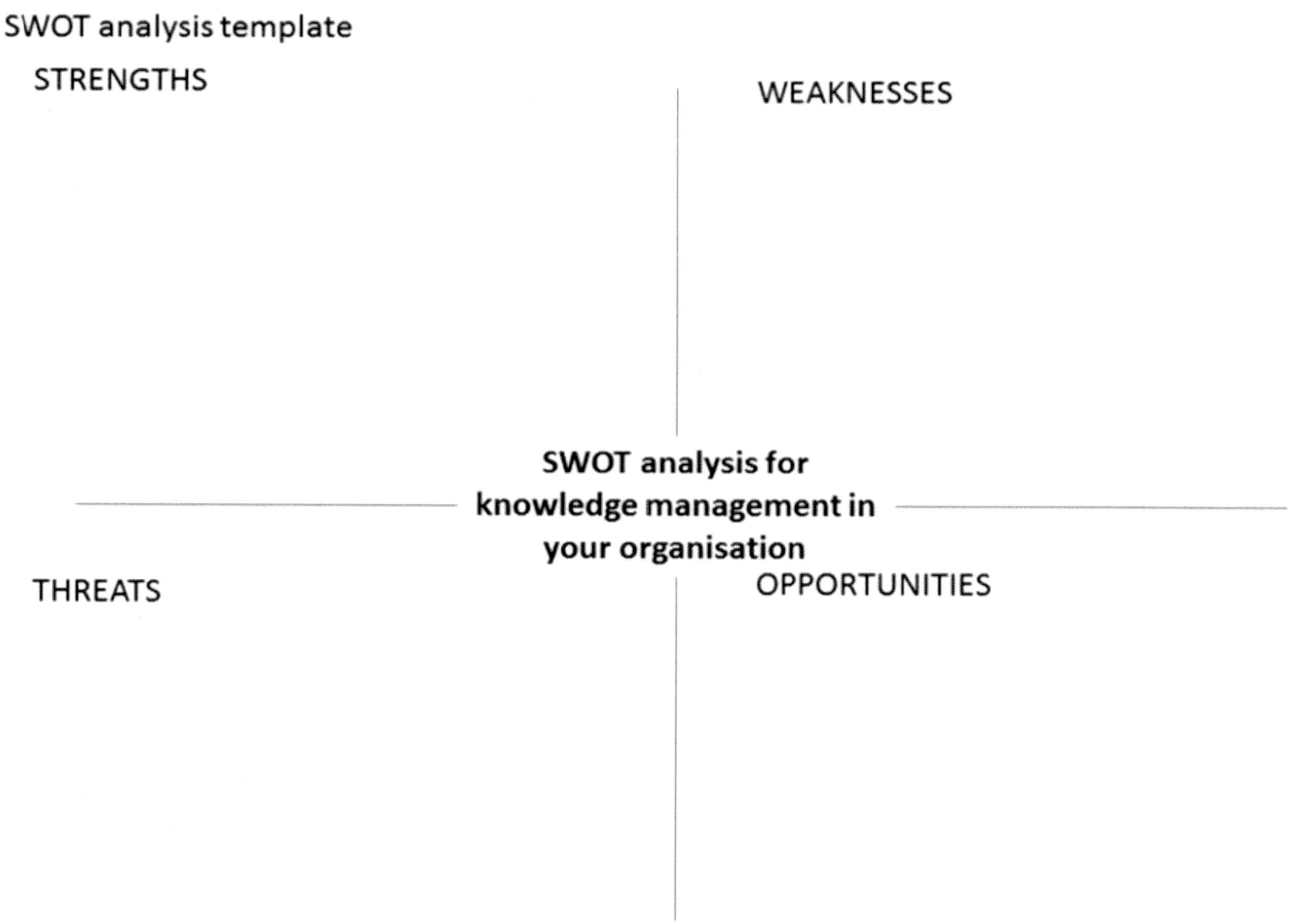

SWOT analysis template

STRENGTHS

WEAKNESSES

SWOT analysis for
knowledge management in
your organisation

OPPORTUNITIES

THREATS

SWOT analysis template

Taken from Chapter 5 Engaging your Team – in "The Effective Team's

Fully Developed Practical Scenarios

The following are the consolidated notes for each of the three scenarios, taken from the various chapters of this book.

Scenario 1: Making changes to a business support group's products or services

Defining your strategy (Chapter 2)

The central library is coordinating the purchase of print and electronic resources, subscriptions and loans on behalf of a network of local libraries. Each of the local libraries interfaces directly with the local business (or functional) groups that it supports.

There are a few ways in which the central and local libraries could pool their knowledge. For instance library staff in the local libraries will have a detailed knowledge of different customer groups and their requirements. Those in the central library will have a specialised knowledge of the processes involved in managing the central resources.

It is likely that all concerned will have strategic goals and objectives relating to the reduction of costs, and the increase of customer satisfaction.

The central library could benefit from the specialised knowledge of members of the local library. One individual might be the key contact, for example, for customers in a field of scientific research or a discipline such as Human Resources.

A potential mind-map is shown in Figure i

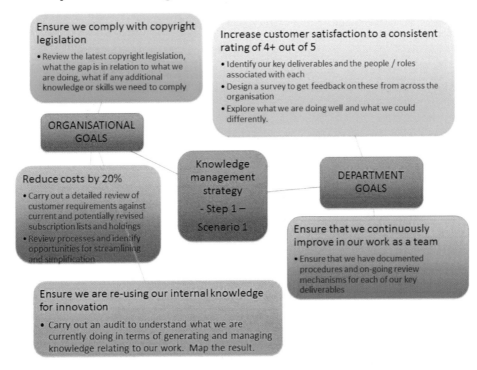

Figure i. A mind-map for the potential knowledge management strategy for Scenario 1

Selecting your tactics (Chapter 3)

The central library could use an Ask the Expert activity with individual members of the local library. This would explore staff members' expertise relating to their customers' requirements and so inform decisions about subscriptions for the next calendar year. This understanding will help to support discussions about how to best manage costs, and how to optimise customer satisfaction.

The central library could also conduct a Peer Assist with peer groups in external, non-competing, libraries to explore alternative, cost-reduction approaches for managing subscriptions and loans.

Library staff in the different local libraries could set up a Community of Practice to explore how best to increase customer satisfaction.

The return on investment in these examples would be a comparison of the time invested in the knowledge sharing activities, compared to the reductions in costs, and the increase in customer satisfaction.

A potential mind-map for these and other knowledge tactics is shown in Figure ii.

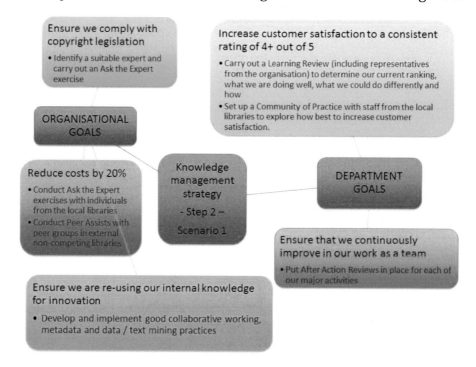

Figure ii. A mind-map for the knowledge tactics for Scenario 1

Engaging your Team (Chapter 5)

The potential knowledge management strategy for this scenario focuses on accessing the specialised knowledge of the staff in the central and local libraries, and learning from the expertise of similar organisations. This would help with the annual review of subscriptions and the streamlining of processes for subscriptions and loans in order to reduce costs and increase customer satisfaction.

Senior managers will be able to ensure that the strategy is reflected in departmental and individual objectives, and that people's performance is evaluated and rewarded accordingly.

Senior and middle managers will also ensure that knowledge-sharing activities are seen as a priority and that time is set aside to carry them out effectively.

Managers might even take part in or attend some of the activities and cite them as examples of good practice when talking to other members of the department or organisation.

The teams involved could document guidelines and then continuously review and improve on them after each round of knowledge sharing is completed so as to benefit from the lessons learned.

The knowledge strategy and how it is progressing could be a standing item on the teams' agendas, to provide updates on progress and the benefits gained.

What happens next? Elevator pitches (Chapter 6)

Here is one way in which the scenario's elevator pitch could be articulated:

"Our library staff in the central and local libraries would like to make better use of their expertise during the annual review of subscriptions and for how they go about subscriptions and loans generally. We will teach and facilitate some exercises that will help them to share their knowledge, and tap into that of external colleagues and so reduce costs and increase customer satisfaction."

Scenario 2 – Enhancing the effectiveness of scientific projects

Defining your strategy (Chapter 2)

The Life Science team carries out internal research projects, and study-related projects for external clients, which are prime opportunities for applying knowledge management.

The long-term strategic objectives that these approaches could be addressing are for example reducing overall costs associated with the projects, reducing cycle time, increasing internal and external customer satisfaction. Short-term benefits might include the avoidance or reduction of risks associated with the project, or the grasping of otherwise unknown or ill-defined opportunities.

A mind-map of the knowledge strategy is shown in Figure iii.

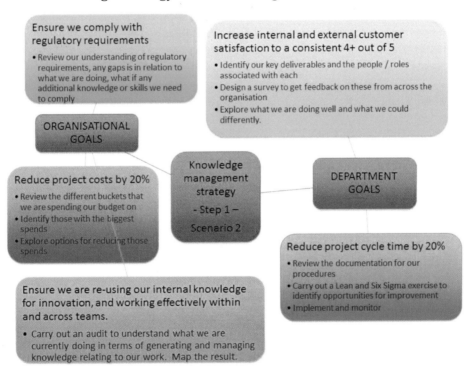

Figure iii. A mind-map for the knowledge management strategy for Scenario 2

Selecting your tactics (Chapter 3)

The Life Science team could:

- Conduct a Peer Assist before starting on a new project to ensure that key learnings from other projects (what to do, or not to do, and how) are considered as part of the project plan and risk assessment.

45

- Hold After Action Reviews at pre-agreed project milestones (sometimes known as key decision points, or gateways) to ensure that any key learnings are being considered before moving onto the next phase.
- Carry out Learning Reviews at the end of projects to reflect on, address and share key learnings arising from this project, and for future ones.

The Life Science team can consolidate its learnings in the form of documented or updated procedures. These can include lessons learnt, hints and tips or even video clips. They can carefully apply metadata to electronic records to facilitate their retrieval. They can also use data mining on existing records to discover new insights.

Teams working in geographically dispersed locations, or even within the same location will benefit from agreed collaborative working practices for managing their electronic information and discussions.

A mind-map of these and other knowledge tactics is shown in Figure iv.

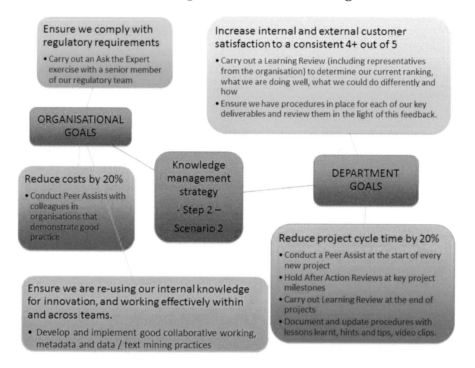

Figure iv. A mind-map for the knowledge tactics for Scenario 2

Engaging your Team (Chapter 5)

The knowledge strategy for this scenario consists of supporting the reduction of overall costs associated with the projects, the reduction of cycle time, and the increase in internal and external customer satisfaction.

There are also short-term benefits to be gained such as avoiding or reducing risks associated with projects, or enabling the grasping of otherwise unknown or ill-defined opportunities.

The strategy includes carrying out learning before, during and after interventions on new, existing and completed projects. It also includes embedding the lessons learned in documented procedures, using metadata to index records, using data mining and developing collaborative working practices.

This is quite a broad range of activities to encourage and support, so the management team could support the strategy by recruiting or training a dedicated knowledge management resource. This resource could be a single person, or a small team depending on the pace and scale at which the organisation would like to progress.

The individual or small team could then work with representatives across the business to develop and then implement the new ways of working. This would be a good way to build success stories or case studies and perhaps to also cultivate opinion leaders to help spread the message across the organisation.

Understanding and adjusting the approach for implementation based on different stakeholders' attitudes and skills will be beneficial.

It will also be important to make the knowledge strategy part of everyone's objectives to ensure that there is a commitment across the board to adopt it.

If there is a small team or a set of representatives is used to design and implement the knowledge strategy, then it will be important to help them achieve high performance.

Some form of team start–up event, with visible endorsement by senior management, will help to do this. The start-up agenda could include:

- Articulating the vision and anticipated benefits
- Developing the plan of approach
- Agreeing how the team will monitor and review progress and generally manage its interactions and activities.

What happens next? Elevator pitches (Chapter 6)

Here is one way in which the scenario's elevator pitch could be articulated:

"Our scientists and senior managers would like to feel confident that they are making the best use of our internal knowledge when initiating and managing projects for external customers. We will coach and support project teams to use learning interventions at the start, during and at the end of all projects so that we can, as far as possible, reduce the cycle time and cost of our projects, and consistently ensure customer satisfaction."

Scenario 3 - Refocusing the approach of an SME (Small or Medium Enterprise)

Defining your strategy (Chapter 2)

This organisation has significant opportunities to grow through the exploitation of internal and external knowledge and expertise. It has a number of different options for how to go about this.

Again, the goals should be expressed first in terms of written objectives such as increasing the SME's market share, its customer base or revenue by x%; being recognized as a centre of excellence in its field of research through rankings, invitations to speak, publications, patents; and so on.

SMEs typically build their knowledge base by recruiting experts to join their Advisory Boards, their senior management and scientific teams. Their staff members attend and speak at conferences, and the SME invites external speakers to give seminars. Staff members read and publish papers. And of course SMEs grow their internal bank of records and databases.

A mind-map for the knowledge strategy is shown in Figure v.

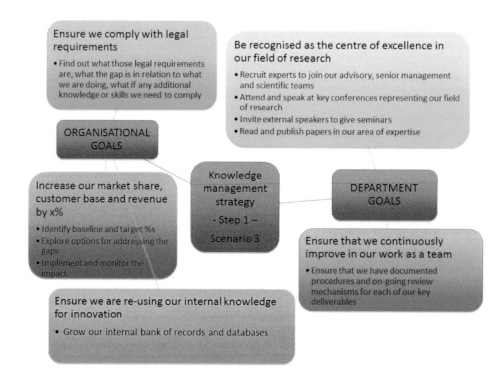

Figure v. A mind-map for the knowledge management strategy for Scenario 3

Knowledge Management techniques that the SME could consider to make better use of its internal and external expertise include:

- Structured Ask the Expert and Peer Assist style conversations
- Thoughtful use of metadata for documenting their records
- Data and text mining on the records of their work
- Encouraging good collaborative working practices within and across teams to optimise how they share their knowledge and information.

As with Scenario 2, the complexity involved might benefit from the support of a dedicated individual or small team with representatives from the different parts of the organisation.

Support from the senior managers will be essential given the significant cultural changed involved to transition from an academic to a more business like organisation. The managers will need to be seen to actively endorse and model the knowledge sharing and collaborative working approaches. They will be expected to act on any escalations of non-conformance, and to acknowledge and reward examples of good practice.

Other tactics include those described for Scenarios 1 and 2 such as:

- The use of explicit performance objectives
- Sharing success stories
- Cultivating opinion leaders
- Developing guidelines for training and support
- Embedding good practices within documented procedures and so on.

A mind-map of these and other knowledge tactics is shown in Figure vi.

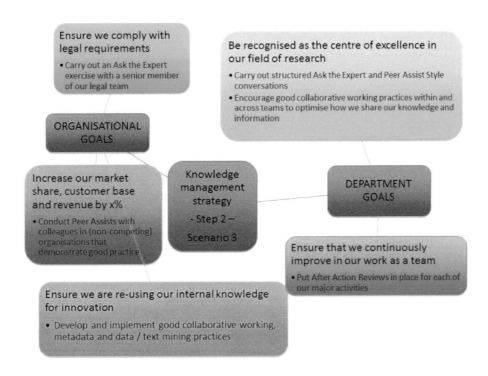

Figure vi. A mind-map for the knowledge tactics for Scenario 3

What happens next? Elevator pitches (Chapter 6)

Here is one way in which the scenario's elevator pitch could be articulated:

"We need to find ways to transition from being an academic to a more business like organisation. We will be introducing a range of knowledge sharing and collaborative approaches that will enable us to make better use of our internal and external expertise in order to facilitate and support that transition."

Further Reading

1. Clemmons Rumizen, Melissi (2002) *The Complete Idiot's Guide to Knowledge Management.* CWL Publishing.

   A very useful, and very readable, overview of everything one might want to know about Knowledge Management.

2. Collison, Chris and Parcell, Geoff (2004) *Learning to Fly.* Second Edition. Capston Publishing.

   A widely acknowledged 'go to' reference point for techniques to use when sharing knowledge between people.

3. Editorial (2016) *Microsoft and AstraZeneca cancer simulation to speed up advent of personalised medicine.* Business Weekly, 22nd September.

   An example of the value of data mining techniques: the article describes the use of computer modeling of signaling pathways to provide scientists with wider choices of hypotheses to investigate than they would otherwise manage.

4. Editorial (2016) *UK technology attractive for global genomics investment.* Business Weekly, 29th September.

   Another example of the value of data mining techniques, applied to large data sets, for those who are not experts in genomics.

5. Goodman, Elisabeth (2013) *Knowledge Management: past, present and future – notes on a NetIKX seminar.* NetIKX http://elisabethgoodman.wordpress.com/2013/03/22/knowledge-management-past-present-and-future-notes-on-a-netikx-seminar-netikx60/ (accessed 20th September 2016).

   A useful overview that does just what the title describes, from a well-established, London-based, network of knowledge practitioners.

6. Goodman, Elisabeth and Riddell, John (2014) *Knowledge Management in the Pharmaceutical Industry – Enhancing Research, Development and Manufacturing Performance.* Gower.

   A comprehensive description of the theory and practice of knowledge management based on the authors' own experience in the Pharmaceutical Industry and that of 27 interviewees. The guidance and advice can be applied in a variety of environments.

7. Gurteen, David (1999) *Creating a knowledge sharing culture.* Knowledge Management Magazine, 2(5).

   Invaluable guidance from a current day international KM practitioner of knowledge cafés and other knowledge sharing conversations.

8. McDermott, Richard, et al (2002) *Cultivating Communities of Practice.* Harvard Business Press.

   Widely recognised as the founder of Communities of Practice.

9. NHS – Health Education England, Knowledge for Healthcare *Knowledge Management Toolkit* http://kfh.libraryservices.nhs.uk/knowledge-management/km-goals-tools-and-techniques/ (accessed 2nd October 2016).

   A very comprehensive, actively maintained resource on knowledge management tools and techniques.

10. Secker, Jane et al (2016) *To boldly go... our role in text and data mining.* CILIP Update, September, pp. 30 – 32.

    An examination of how librarians can facilitate the use of text and data mining by their research customers.